© 2015 Tiddely pom.
The book author retains sole copyright to his or her contributions to this book.
Every effort has been made to locate copyright and permission information.

Visit Tiddely pom online at tiddelypom.com.au

All rights reserved.

ISBN: 978-0-9942928-2-7

Published by Tiddely pom

Rattle and Rumble

by Susan Searle and Jenny Wood

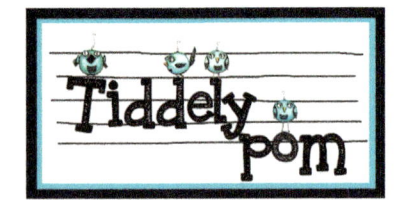

Tiddely pom

ABOUT OUR BOOKS

The Tiddely Songbook project is a collection of music teaching picture books based on traditional children's folk songs and chants. Each book incorporates a pictorial representation of the music alongside formal notation, for children who are preparing to read music. The musical concepts within the illustrations lead children to discover the relationships between sounds and the patterns they form.

The Tiddely Songbooks are to be used by music specialists, pre-school and primary classroom teachers and music-minded parents. The selected songs and rhymes are standards of the Early Years and are a pleasure to read and to sing.

Notes at the end of each book include an overview of the musical content of the song and ways to use the book within a music class.

Additional resources, including a sound recording is available on our website: tiddelypom.com.au

Here it comes with a

rattle and a rumble

Can you hear the whistle blow?

Here it comes with a

rattle and a rumble.

Jump on the train and off we go.

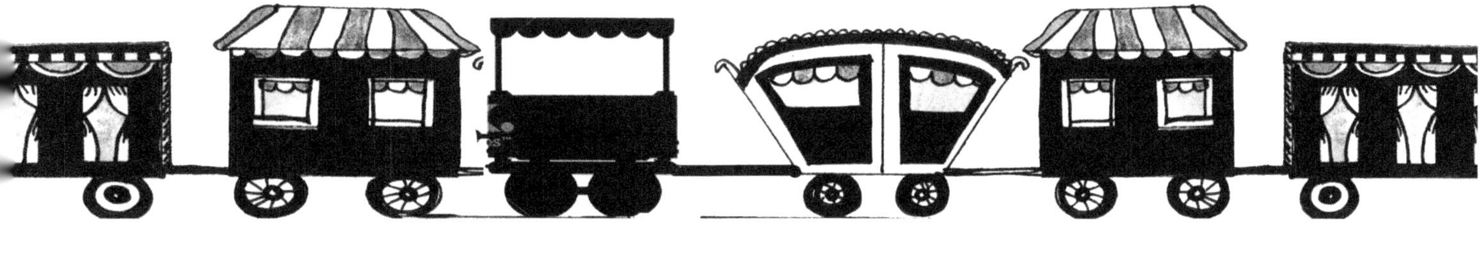

14 Here it comes with a

ratt - le and a rum - ble.

Can you hear the whis - tle blow?

18 Here it comes with a

rattle and a rumble.

20 Jump on the train and off we go!

NOTES ON THE SONG

Here it comes with a rattle and a rumble. Can you hear the whistle blow?

Here it comes with a rattle and a rumble. Jump on the train and off we go!

Note: A sound recording of *Rattle and Rumble* is available on our website: tiddelypom.com.au

Tone set: s,l,t,drm	Comfortable starting pitch: G-A
Appropriate age: 4-7	Rhythmic elements:

PURPOSE

- discover melodic contour: pattern of sounds
- experience descending scale
- discover connection between sounds and visual representation
- develop in-tune singing voice
- early "reading" practice of visual symbols (follow up activity)
- practise musical form

THEMATIC LINKS (related topics)

- Trains, Transport
- Travelling
- Direction: up and down

Literature (some thematically linked picture story books) :

Locomotive:Brian Floca

The Little Engine that Could:Watty Piper

The Little Train:Lois Lensky

Steam Train, Dream Train: Sherrie Duskey Rinker/ Tom Lichtenheld

NOTES FOR TEACHERS

This book allows students to hear music while seeing it in visual form, both in representational pictures and in formal notation. Through this discovery method, they prepare for learning to read and write music themselves. Sharing the books more than once over a period of time will allow students to absorb more and more of the musical concepts within and become independent singers of the song.

SUGGESTED USE

PREPARATION

Enjoy singing the song Rattle and Rumble with hand actions to match the high and low and descending sounds.

SING AND SHOW *THE RATTLE AND RUMBLE* **BOOK**

A steady pace will allow you to turn pages slowly enough for students to absorb the information on each page.

AFTERWARDS

Ask students to share any observations: they may notice something interesting in the artwork or else they may observe a connection between the sounds in the song and the representative notation. Students who have already begun to learn an instrument may notice the formal notation.
If students don't comment on the music notation, don't tell them; let them discover it themselves next time!

FOLLOW UP ACTIVITIES

Students watch and sing as the song is performed for them on a chime bar tone ladder, or upended xylophone (low notes at the bottom, of course!) They will see the high/low and descending sounds modelled on the instrument.

Play an echo game. Play Rattle and Rumble in short phrases, making sure they can't see the instrument. Students must echo the correct phrase.

Eg teacher plays:

students sing:

Can you hear the whist - le blow?

Play the phrases in a mixed up order, so they won't be able to guess what to sing, but will identify the text to match the melody. Repeat some phrases several times to make it trickier.

Display the four phrases visually represented on four cards.* Show the cards out of order and have students place them into the right order to form the song. Sing the cards in the mixed up order before re-ordering them.

Another day, sing Rattle and Rumble in a mixed up order, eg

> Jump on the train and off we go!
> Here it comes with a ratt-le and a rum-ble
> Here it comes with a ratt-le and a rum-ble
> Can you hear the whistle blow?

Students must listen and work as a group to place the cards into the order they hear.

*see www.tiddleypom.com.au for free downloadable cards

ABOUT JENNY AND SUSAN

The Tiddely Songbook project is a collaborative endeavour between two sisters.

Susan Searle is a classroom music teacher, choral director and lecturer in Kodály methodology. With 30 years experience in state and private schools around Melbourne, from ELC to Year 6 in single sex boys and girls and in co-educational settings, she enjoys exploring the wonderful heritage of children's literacy to enrich music lessons for students of all ages.

Jenny Wood is an Australian artist and illustrator who explores both whimsical and classical styles of art. A computer geek by profession, Jenny has studied Fine Art at Curtin University and Illustration at NMIT. She has contributed her talent to countless projects including the illustration of several children's books. She is excited to be working with her sister, Susan on this project.

Jennys' artistic expression and signature style can be viewed on her website.
Website: http://jennywoodart.com/

Tiddely pom